Conquering
THE PEAK OF SUCCESS

A Journey of Reaching Life's Highest Altitudes

ADRIANA OCAMPO SENIOR

A Journey of Reaching Life's Highest Altitudes

©Copyright 2024, Adriana Ocampo Senior.
All rights reserved.

No portion of this book may be reproduced by mechanical, photographic, or electronic process; nor may it be stored in a retrieval system, transmitted in any form, or otherwise be copied for public use or private use without written permission of the copyright owner.

It is sold with the understanding that the publisher and the individual author are not engaged in the rendering of psychological, legal, accounting, or other professional advice.

The content and views in this book are the sole expression and opinion of the author and not necessarily the views of Fig Factor Media, LLC.

For More Information:
Fig Factor Media | figfactormedia.com

Cover Design by Marco Alvarez
Layout by LDG Juan Manuel Serna Rosales

Printed in the United States of America

ISBN: 978-1-959989-94-3
Library of Congress Control Number: 2024917638

Dedication

To the special people in my life who have supported, inspired, and motivated me, this book is a testament to your unwavering belief in my journey. Your encouragement and love have made this story possible, and for that, I am eternally grateful.

Acknowledgments

I would like to extend my deepest gratitude to everyone who has played a part in the creation of this book. To my family members and close friends, your unwavering support has been the backbone of my journey. Your encouragement, patience, and understanding have provided me with the strength to keep pushing forward, even during the most challenging times. Special thanks to my two brothers, whose unconditional love and belief in my abilities have been my guiding light. Your constant reassurance has given me the courage to chase my dreams.

To my mentors and female leaders, *hermanas*, your wisdom and guidance have been invaluable. Your insights and constructive feedback have helped to shape this book into what it is today. I am especially grateful to my editor, whose meticulous attention to detail and commitment to excellence have elevated my work. To my readers, thank you for giving life to these pages with your curiosity and open hearts. It is my hope that this book inspires and resonates with you as much as the journey of creating it has inspired me.

Introduction

Success is a multifaceted concept, often defined by personal goals, professional achievements, and the balance between the two. It means different things to different people, but at its core, success is about setting and achieving meaningful goals that bring fulfillment and happiness. For many, success encompasses not only career milestones but also personal growth, relationships, and contributions to society. In the workplace, particularly for women, and especially women of color, success often involves navigating unique challenges and breaking barriers while striving for professional excellence and personal satisfaction. Preparing for success, especially for women in the workplace, requires a combination of education, resilience, and strategic networking.

Education lays the foundation, equipping you women with the knowledge and skills necessary to excel in our own chosen fields. Continuous learning and professional development are crucial, as they keep you adaptable and competitive in a rapidly changing job market.

Resilience is equally important; it enables women to persevere through setbacks and challenges, turning obstacles into opportunities for growth.

Strategic networking is another critical component. Building a strong support system of mentors, peers, and advocates can provide guidance, open doors, and offer encouragement. Mentorship, in particular, can be a powerful tool, offering insights and advice from those who have already navigated similar paths. Networking also helps in building a personal brand and establishing a presence within an industry, which can lead to new opportunities and collaborations.

In addition, ***self-confidence*** and ***assertiveness*** are essential for women aiming for success in the workplace. Women must believe in their capabilities and advocate for themselves, whether it's negotiating salaries, seeking promotions, or voicing innovative ideas. Cultivating these traits can help overcome biases and stereotypes that may exist in the workplace.

Ultimately, success for women in the workplace is about creating a career that aligns with their ***values*** and ***aspirations,*** while also contributing to a more inclusive and equitable environment for future generations. By preparing strategically, staying resilient, and leveraging the power of networks, women can achieve their goals and redefine success on their own terms.

Transcend

Clear Goals Equal a Clear Road Ahead

Setting clear goals is the cornerstone of achieving success and transcending limitations. When you define your objectives with precision, you create a roadmap that guides your actions and decisions. Clear goals provide direction and purpose, helping you to focus your energy and resources on what truly matters. They act as a compass, steering you through the complexities and distractions of everyday life, ensuring that every step you take is aligned with your ultimate aspirations.

For women in the workplace, having clear goals is especially empowering. It allows you to articulate your ambitions and track your progress, making it easier to navigate the unique challenges you may face. Whether you're aspiring to a leadership role, seeking to balance career and personal life, or aiming to make a significant impact in your field, well-defined goals keep you motivated and resilient. They turn abstract dreams into actionable plans, breaking down daunting tasks into manageable milestones. This clarity not only boosts your confidence but also strengthens your ability to communicate your vision, attracting the support and resources needed to achieve your goals.

In fact, clear goals are the foundation of a clear road ahead. They provide the structure and clarity necessary to transcend obstacles and to reach new heights. By setting specific, measurable, achievable, relevant, and time-bound (SMART) goals, you create a pathway to success that is both inspiring and attainable. This strategic approach to goal setting empowers you to transcend the ordinary and achieve the extraordinary, paving the way for a fulfilling and impactful career.

Building Your Skills

Building your skills is a fundamental aspect of personal and professional growth, enabling you to stay competitive and to adapt to an ever-evolving workplace. Skill development is not just about acquiring new knowledge; it's about refining existing abilities and expanding your expertise to meet the demands of your career. Whether it's mastering the latest technology, improving your communication capabilities, or honing your leadership qualities, continuous learning is the key to unlocking new opportunities and achieving success.

For women in the workplace, building skills can be particularly transformative. It empowers you to break through barriers and challenge stereotypes, demonstrating your competence and potential. Investing in skill development shows a commitment to excellence and a proactive approach to career advancement. By seeking out training programs, workshops, and professional certifications, you can enhance your qualifications and position yourself as a valuable asset within your organization. Moreover, developing a diverse skill set allows you to pivot and to seize new opportunities, ensuring long-term career resilience.

In addition to formal education, practical experience and on-the-job learning are crucial components of skill building. Taking on challenging projects, seeking mentorship, and engaging in collaborative efforts can significantly enhance your abilities. These experiences provide real-world applications of your skills, fostering growth through practice and feedback. Networking with peers and industry leaders also offers invaluable insights and can lead to new learning opportunities and collaborations.

Ultimately, building your skills is an ongoing journey that requires dedication, curiosity, and a willingness to step outside your comfort zone. By continuously enhancing your capabilities, you not only advance your career but also inspire others to pursue their own growth. This commitment to personal and professional development paves the way for a successful and fulfilling career, empowering you to make meaningful contributions and transcend the limitations of the past.

Demonstrating Reliability and Accountability

Reliability and accountability are cornerstones of professional success, laying the foundation for trust and respect in the workplace. Demonstrating these qualities means consistently delivering on promises, meeting deadlines, and maintaining a high standard of work. When colleagues and supervisors can depend on you to follow through on your commitments, you build a reputation as a reliable and trustworthy team member. This not only enhances your credibility but also fosters a positive work environment where collaboration and mutual support can thrive.

For women in the workplace, showcasing reliability and accountability is particularly impactful. It can help to counteract any biases or doubts about your capabilities, proving through consistent actions that you are a dependable and competent professional. By taking ownership of your responsibilities and holding yourself accountable for your performance, you set a powerful example for others and demonstrate leadership potential. This proactive attitude signals that you are committed to your role and the success of your team, earning you greater respect and more opportunities for advancement.

Accountability goes beyond just completing tasks; it involves taking responsibility for your actions and their outcomes. This means being honest about mistakes, learning from them, and making the necessary adjustments to prevent them in the future. Embracing accountability fosters a growth mindset, where challenges are seen as opportunities for improvement rather than setbacks. It also encourages open communication and transparency, which are essential for effective teamwork and problem-solving.

In essence, demonstrating reliability and accountability not only bolsters your professional reputation but also contributes to a culture of trust and integrity within your organization. By consistently showing that you can be counted on to deliver quality work and to take responsibility for your actions, you position yourself as a key player in your team's success. This commitment to reliability and accountability paves the way for career growth, helping you to transcend professional challenges and achieve your goals.

Transcending the Andes Mountains

In December 2021, I had the amazing magical experience of running the Patagonian Mountains, crossing the Andes Mountains from Argentina to Chile, on a three-day adventure, with runners from forty-five different countries around the globe. The event, called "El Cruce," is all about being different. Participants get to immerse themselves in the mountains from the very start of the race. The chosen routes are very challenging and demand significant physical exertion; therefore, it is essential to *train conscientiously* prior to the race.

Months before the race, I attended a few webinars with expert runners and previous participants to learn and to prepare for the competition and the mandatory equipment that must be carried throughout all three stages of the race. Also, about the non-essential, but recommended, equipment that, eventually, significantly helped enhance my race experience.

Preparation is key! Runners' bags had to be dropped off one day before the start of the race. Having a checklist in hand really served as a helpful guide to ensure I had all the essentials while assembling my bag in preparation for the race.

Influence and Inspire

Creating Your Support System

Creating a robust support system is essential for both personal and professional growth. A strong network of supportive individuals provides guidance, encouragement, and resources that can significantly impact your success. This support system can include mentors, colleagues, friends, and family members who understand your goals and are invested in your progress. By surrounding yourself with people who believe in you and your vision, you create an environment that fosters confidence, resilience, and motivation.

For women in the workplace, building a support system is especially crucial. Mentors and sponsors can offer invaluable advice and open doors to new opportunities, helping you to navigate the complexities of your career. Colleagues can provide feedback, share experiences, and collaborate on projects, creating a sense of camaraderie and shared purpose. Family and friends offer emotional support, helping to balance the demands of work and personal life. Actively seeking out and nurturing these relationships ensures you have a diverse network of allies to turn to in times of need and celebration.

Developing a support system requires intentional effort and reciprocity. It's important to actively engage with your network, offering support in return and building mutually beneficial relationships. Attend industry events, join professional organizations, and participate in networking opportunities to connect with like-minded individuals. Foster these connections through regular communication, showing genuine interest in their journeys and achievements. By investing time and energy into building your support system, you create a foundation that not only aids in your success but also enriches your professional and personal life.

Basically, a strong support system is a powerful tool for influence and inspiration. It provides the encouragement and resources needed to overcome challenges and to seize opportunities. By surrounding yourself with supportive and inspiring individuals, you enhance your ability to achieve your goals and to make a positive impact on those around you. This network of allies and mentors becomes an integral part of your journey, empowering you to reach new heights and inspire others along the way.

Empowering Those Around You

Empowering those around you is a vital aspect of leadership and personal fulfillment. It involves creating an environment where individuals feel valued, supported, and capable of achieving their best. By fostering a culture of empowerment, you encourage others to take initiative, express their ideas, and develop their skills. This not only enhances team performance but also builds a foundation of trust and mutual respect. When people feel empowered, they are more likely to contribute creatively, to take ownership of their work, and to collaborate effectively.

For women in the workplace, empowering others can be particularly transformative. It involves advocating for equal opportunities, providing mentorship, and actively supporting the growth and development of colleagues. By recognizing and celebrating the achievements of others, you create a positive and inclusive work environment. Sharing knowledge and offering guidance helps to build confidence and competence in those around you. This collaborative approach not only strengthens the team but also paves the way for more diverse and innovative solutions.

Empowerment also involves creating opportunities for others to shine. This means delegating responsibilities, encouraging professional development, and promoting a culture of continuous learning. By trusting others with important tasks and projects, you demonstrate confidence in their abilities and help them to build their own leadership skills. Providing constructive feedback and recognizing contributions further reinforces their sense of value and capability.

Empowering those around you is about fostering a supportive and dynamic work environment where everyone can thrive. It requires empathy, active listening, and a commitment to nurturing the potential in others. By empowering your colleagues, you not only enhance their personal and professional growth, but also contribute to a more collaborative and innovative workplace. This approach creates a ripple effect, inspiring others to adopt the same empowering mindset and ultimately leading to a more engaged and successful team.

Celebrate Achievements

Celebrating achievements is a powerful way to acknowledge hard work, recognize success, and foster a culture of positivity and appreciation. Whether it's reaching a milestone, completing a project, or overcoming a challenge, taking the time to celebrate accomplishments is essential for morale and motivation. It not only boosts confidence and morale but also reinforces the value of effort and dedication. By celebrating achievements, you create a sense of pride and fulfillment within your team, inspiring them to continue striving for excellence.

For women in the workplace, celebrating achievements holds particular significance. It offers an opportunity to shine a spotlight on their contributions and accomplishments, while combating imposter syndrome and promoting self-confidence. Recognizing the achievements of female colleagues helps to break down barriers and stereotypes, demonstrating the importance of diversity and inclusion in the workplace. It also sends a powerful message about the value of women's leadership and expertise, inspiring future generations to pursue their goals fearlessly.

Celebrating achievements can take many forms, from simple acknowledgments to more elaborate ceremonies or events. It's not just about the outcome but also the journey and the effort that went into it. Whether it's a team lunch, a heartfelt thank-you message, or a public recognition ceremony, the key is to make individuals feel valued and appreciated for their contributions. This fosters a sense of belonging and camaraderie within the team, strengthening relationships and promoting collaboration.

In essence, celebrating achievements is about more than just patting ourselves on the back; it's about fostering a culture of gratitude, recognition, and positivity. By taking the time to celebrate accomplishments, we not only boost morale and motivation but also inspire continued growth and success. It's a reminder that every step forward, no matter how small, deserves to be acknowledged and celebrated.

Inspiration in the Andes

The crossing of the Andes Mountains was initiated in the town of Villa La Angostura in Argentina. The total distance of the race was 100 kilometers, divided into three states. The places where the event took place was of unparalleled beauty. The runners crossed mountains, volcanoes, snow-capped peaks, forests, lakes, valleys, and rocky areas.

The last of the race, stage 3, we climbed 1,861 meter above sea level to Cerro O'Connor, with a positive elevation of 1,586 meters. It took me 3:42 hours to reach the mountain top. The view from the highest point was breathtaking.

As everyone was taking pictures and videos, I noticed one lady who was rather nervous and not enjoying the moment like the rest of us, so I approached her to offer my help and to start a conversation. The lady was from Mexico and had traveled to Argentina to do the race with her sister. She admitted that although she exercises frequently, she is not a runner or a climber, and had not trained properly for the race. She also shared that she suffers from acrophobia, a type of specific phobia that involves an intense fear of heights. Acrophobia causes people to feel extremely fearful and anxious about situations that involve being far off the ground. Therefore, she could not look down to enjoy the beautiful view of the mountains, valleys, and rivers. More importantly, she was afraid of coming down the mountain.

I approached an experienced runner from Argentina, who I had met along the path. She had competed before and knew the mountains and the terrain well. I explained the situation and between the two of us, we helped the Mexican lady get to the bottom of the mountain. At that point, we didn't care about our own timing anymore. The focus was about helping our fellow female runner in a moment of vulnerability.

Facing our fears is crucial for personal growth, as it allows us to break free from the limitations they impose. By acknowledging and confronting what frightens us, we not only empower ourselves but also open the door to vulnerability. Trusting others to support us in this journey can foster connection and understanding, reminding us that we don't have to face challenges alone. Together, we can navigate the path to resilience, turning fears into opportunities for transformation and deeper relationships.

At the end of each day, we got to rest at two incredible camp locations, nestled in nature, where we experienced camaraderie with the other runners. Although I traveled with three close friends, I did not see them during the race, as all left in different groups. Having the ability to travel solo, to communicate well with others, and to be comfortable while being uncomfortable made a huge difference!

Ascend

Persistence and Resilience

Persistence and resilience are the bedrock of success, guiding us through the inevitable challenges and setbacks that arise on the path to our goals. In the face of adversity, it's our ability to persevere and bounce back that ultimately determines our trajectory. Persistence is the unwavering commitment to continue striving for our aspirations, even when faced with obstacles or failures. It's about maintaining focus and determination, refusing to be deterred by setbacks or naysayers. Resilience, on the other hand, is the capacity to adapt and to recover from adversity, emerging stronger and tougher than before. It's the willingness to learn from setbacks, cultivate inner strength, and embrace challenges as opportunities for growth.

For women in the workplace, persistence and resilience are particularly critical. Despite significant strides towards gender equality, women still face unique challenges and biases in the professional world. Persistence allows women to push through barriers, to advocate for themselves, and to pursue their ambitions with unwavering determination. It's about refusing to accept limitations imposed by others and forging ahead with confidence and conviction. Resilience, meanwhile, helps women navigate the ups and downs of their careers, bouncing back from setbacks and using adversity as fuel for personal and professional growth. It's about recognizing that failure is not a reflection of our worth but rather an opportunity to learn, to adapt, and to come back even stronger.

Together, persistence and resilience form the foundation for ascending to new heights in our personal and professional lives. They enable us to overcome challenges, to seize opportunities, and to achieve our full potential. By cultivating these qualities, we not only empower ourselves but also inspire others to persevere in the face of adversity. As we ascend to new heights, let us remember that it's not the absence of challenges that defines our success but rather our response to them. With persistence and resilience as our guiding principles, there's no limit to what we can achieve.

Adaptability

Adaptability is the ability to adjust to new circumstances, to embrace change, and to thrive in dynamic environments. In today's rapidly evolving world, the ability to adapt is more important than ever, as industries, technologies, and work environments undergo constant transformation. Adaptability is not just about reacting to change; it's about proactively seeking out opportunities for growth and innovation. It involves being open-minded, flexible, and willing to step outside of your comfort zone in order to navigate challenges and seize new opportunities.

For women in the workplace, adaptability is a valuable asset that can help overcome systemic barriers and biases. It enables women to navigate shifting expectations, break through glass ceilings, and carve out their own paths to success. By embracing change and staying agile in the face of adversity, women can leverage their unique perspectives and experiences to drive innovation and to lead with confidence. Adaptability also empowers women to balance competing priorities, such as career advancement, family responsibilities, and personal growth, without compromising their values or well-being.

In addition to personal growth, adaptability is essential for building resilient and high-performing teams. When individuals are able to adapt to change, they can collaborate more effectively, communicate more openly, and problem-solve more creatively. By fostering a culture of adaptability within organizations, leaders can cultivate a workforce that is better equipped to navigate uncertainty and capitalize on emerging opportunities. This not only drives innovation and growth but also creates a more inclusive and supportive work environment where everyone can thrive.

Fundamentally, adaptability is a skill that empowers women to overcome obstacles, to seize opportunities, and to thrive in an ever-changing world. By embracing change and staying agile, women can unlock their full potential and lead with confidence, resilience, and innovation. As we continue to navigate the complexities of the modern workplace, let us remember that adaptability is not just a survival skill—it's a key driver of success and growth in our personal and professional lives.

Self-Discipline

Self-discipline is the cornerstone of personal and professional success, providing the inner strength and focus needed to achieve our goals. It is the ability to regulate our thoughts, emotions, and actions in pursuit of a greater purpose, even in the face of distractions or temptations. Self-discipline is about making deliberate choices that align with our long-term objectives, rather than succumbing to immediate gratification or short-term impulses. It requires dedication, perseverance, and a commitment to excellence in everything we do.

For women in the workplace, self-discipline is particularly empowering. It enables women to overcome systemic barriers and biases by demonstrating their competence, reliability, and dedication. By setting high standards for themselves and holding themselves accountable, women can break through glass ceilings and achieve their full potential. Self-discipline also helps women navigate the complexities of work-life balance, allowing them to prioritize their professional and personal responsibilities without sacrificing their well-being or values.

Moreover, self-discipline is essential for building resilience and adaptability in the face of challenges. When we cultivate self-discipline, we develop the mental fortitude needed to persevere through setbacks, overcome obstacles, and bounce back from failure. This inner strength not only fuels our personal growth but also inspires others to follow our lead. By embodying self-discipline, women can serve as role models for their colleagues and future generations, demonstrating the power of focus, determination, and perseverance in achieving success.

Essentially, self-discipline is a fundamental skill that empowers women to unlock their full potential and to lead with confidence and integrity. By cultivating self-discipline, women can overcome barriers, seize opportunities, and make a lasting impact in their careers and communities. As we strive for excellence in all aspects of our lives, let us remember that self-discipline is not just a means to an end—it is a lifelong journey of growth, self-discovery, and empowerment.

Ascending the Andes Mountains

On the first day of the race, we covered Cerro Bayo, for a distance of 28 kilometers, then passed through the Correntoso River and ended at the Lago Espejo camping site.

On day two, we started from Camp 1 itself. The second stage distance was of 23 kilometers, arriving at Camp Inalco, a place that was undoubtedly impressive.

For the third and last stage, the distance was 28 kilometers, and the highlight was Cerro O'Connor which gave us incredible views. After helping the Mexican lady come down the hill, I was exhausted and my left knee was in a lot of pain. Once we made it to the valley, I remember seeing the aid station at a distance and thought to myself, "This is it, I cannot go any further than here. I will ask at the aid station for pain medicine, to be removed from the race, and be taken back to Villa La Angostura."

The volunteer at the aid station checked my knee and reassured me that it wasn't injured. He gave me a pain pill and told me I was only 7 kilometers away from the finish line, with a flat road ahead. He encouraged me to keep going and not give up. I remember him mentioning how many people who had started the race had to quit, and that I was so close to finishing as a winner! He reminded me to think about WHY I started—not just to WISH for it, but to WORK for it, to WORK hard and be PROUD. And that was exactly what I needed. Those words of encouragement were my fuel and my healing medicine. I got off that chair and started running!

I remember passing a man who could hardly walk, supported by his wife as she helped him along. He was in much worse condition than I was, yet he never thought about stopping or giving up. His first-born son was waiting for him on the other side of the finish line. That moment reminded me to put things into perspective. I had been ready to give up the race when my situation wasn't nearly as dire. I'm so grateful to the volunteer at the aid station who reminded me of the importance of perseverance.

In times of difficulty, persistence becomes our greatest ally. When faced with challenges, it's easy to feel overwhelmed and consider giving up, but it's during these moments that our true strength is revealed. By pushing through adversity, we cultivate resilience and gain valuable insights that can only be forged through hardship. Each step taken in the face of difficulty not only brings us closer to our goals but also builds our character, teaching us the value of commitment and grit. Ultimately, embracing persistence allows us to transform setbacks into stepping stones for future success.

About the Author

As a dynamic leader, visionary consultant, and captivating speaker with over twenty-five years of experience in the aerospace industry, Adriana Ocampo Senior helps women, Latinas, and organizations unlock their full potential. With a wealth of experience and a passion for guiding others, Adriana offers innovative consulting services, personalized coaching, and inspiring keynote speeches that leave a lasting impact.

Adriana is a contributing author of the *Hispanic Stars Rising Vol. II,* compiled by Claudia Romo Edelman, and also, of *Latinas in Aviation Vol. IV* compiled by Jacqueline S. Ruiz.

Adriana has received numerous awards, including the Great Minds in STEM (GMiS) "Luminary Award", the Women of Color in Technology "All-Star Award", and the Society of Hispanic Professional Engineers (SHPE) "Rod Garcia Founders STAR Award", a recognition of her outstanding skills, expertise, and knowledge.

Adriana is the current president of the Dallas/Fort Worth Hispanic 100 Latina Leaders organization and also serves on the board of High-Tech High Heels of North Texas. She is a lifetime member and former board member of the Society of Hispanic Professional Engineers (SHPE). In 2024, she established The Ocampo-Senior STEM Scholarship to support Hispanic female college students wanting to pursue studies in STEM fields.

Adriana holds a bachelor of science in industrial engineering from the University of Missouri-Columbia, and a master of business administration degree from Maryville University.

CONTACT HER AT:

Adriana@AdrianaOcampoSenior or visit *www.AdrianaOcampoSenior.com*

www.ingramcontent.com/pod-product-compliance
Lightning Source LLC
Chambersburg PA
CBHW041414010526
44107CB00016B/1167